TO SAMANTHA

[signature]
2006

CONNOR

THE CARVER
CARVES MICHIGAN'S SYMBOLS
By
Gary Elzerman

Illustrated By
Mark J. Herrick

To my wife, Paula, and my children, Connor and Nicole.
Thanks for all the love and inspiration you have given me.

To Edna Cucksey Stephens for her vision and hard work
in developing the book concept and manuscript.

To Mark Herrick for his wonderful illustrations.

To the fantastic EDCO Publishing staff for their kindness and consideration.

To Christopher Pirrone for the great photographs of the carved symbols.

To Ron Pirrone for his help and guidance through all my adventures.

To Mom and Dad, thank you for everything.
G.E.

To the children, may you learn more about about the great state of Michigan.
M.H.

EDCO Publishing, Inc.
2648 Lapeer Rd.
Auburn Hills, MI 48326
www.edcopublishing.com

ISBN-13: 978-0-9749412-7-1

ISBN-10: 0-9749412-7-1

Library of Congress Control Number: 2005933638

Printed in the United States of America by Mitchell Graphics, Petoskey, Michigan

This book is not an instruction manual. Anyone who desires to pursue or encourage an interest in
any aspect of or similar to the wood carving process, tools or techniques mentioned in this book,
should seek the advice and instruction of a professional.

Children should not attempt to use chainsaws or any process, tool and/or carving techniques in this
book. Adults and organizations who provide this book to children, should instruct them that the
chainsaw carvings in this book should not be attempted in any way by children.

EQUIPMENT AND SAFETY

Tools *ARE NOT* toys!

These tools are used by adults <u>ONLY</u>!

Long Chainsaw
To cut a rough, simple shape

Medium Chainsaw
To carve a basic shape

Small Chainsaw
To make detailed cuts

Electric Screw Gun
For securing a wood block to the carving stump

Power Sander
For detailing and smoothing carvings

Propane Torch
For highlighting and adding color and depth to carvings

Chainsaw Blades

CONNOR'S STUDIO

1
2
3
4
5
6

Connor's motto is "Safety First"!

He is very careful when using chainsaws and other tools and ... he dresses for safety, too!

CONNOR'S PERSONAL SAFETY GEAR

1. Protective eyewear
2. Hearing protection and radio
3. Jacket
4. Protective leather gloves
5. Protective leg chaps
6. Heavy steel-toed boots

"Michigan, My Michigan!"

Hi, I'm *Connor* and this is my dog, Riley!

"**Michigan** has many beautiful places. One of my favorite places to visit is the State Capitol in Lansing.

"The Capitol building was designed by architect Elijah Meyers, the greatest designer of capitol buildings in American history. Michigan's Capitol became the model for many other state capitols.

"After Meyers designed the Capitol, many artists worked together to complete this beautiful, historic building in 1879.

"I'm an artist too, but I don't use paints, brushes, plaster, stone, metal or clay like the artists who built the Capitol.

The *State Flag* was adopted in 1911. It is the image of the state's Coat of Arms on a blue background.

"In my studio, I use photographs, memories of what I have seen, my imagination, and a chainsaw to create art sculptures from logs. My name is Connor the Carver. Join my loyal dog, Riley, and me as we explore some of Michigan's beautiful places and carve the state symbols.

"In our travels, you will discover many interesting facts about our great state, it's symbols and why it is a special place to live, work and play."

Michigan became the *26th state* in 1837. *Lansing* was named the capital city ten years later.

Connor and Riley traveled about 90 miles, one-way, from their home in Oxford, Michigan, to visit the State Capitol. How many miles is Lansing from your home?

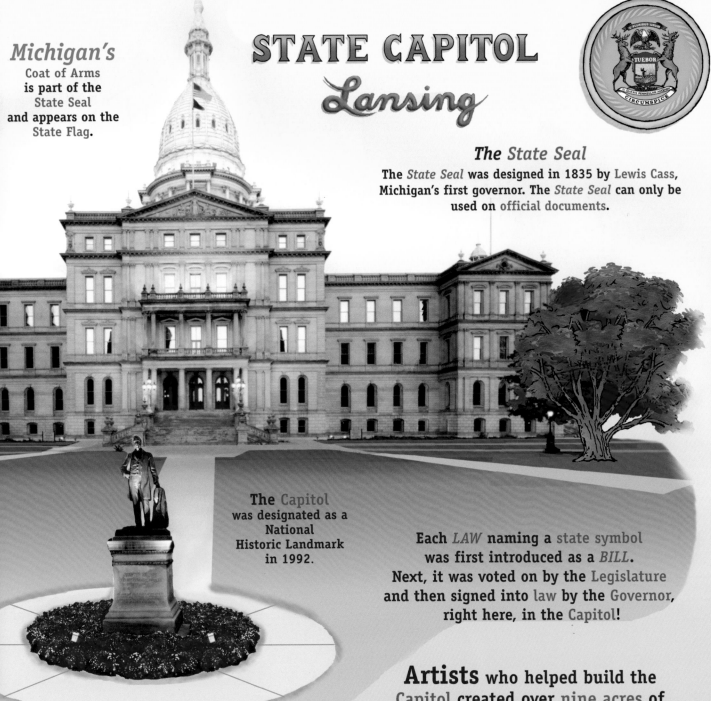

Michigan's Coat of Arms is part of the State Seal and appears on the State Flag.

STATE CAPITOL
Lansing

The State Seal
The *State Seal* was designed in 1835 by Lewis Cass, Michigan's first governor. The *State Seal* can only be used on official documents.

The Capitol was designated as a National Historic Landmark in 1992.

Each *LAW* naming a state symbol was first introduced as a *BILL*. Next, it was voted on by the Legislature and then signed into law by the Governor, right here, in the Capitol!

Artists who helped build the Capitol created over nine acres of hand-painted walls, ceilings, doors, windows, wainscot and columns. Plaster, pine and cast iron were hand painted to look like more expensive marble and walnut.

The bronze statue in front of the Capitol commemorates Austin Blair, *Michigan's Civil War Governor.* He served the state from 1861-1864. Over 90,000 Michigan troops fought for the Union during the Civil War. Blair helped to abolish slavery in the U.S. He was also a leader for *equal rights for women*.

Over 200,000 people visit Michigan's Capitol each year.

APPLE BLOSSOM - State Flower

Michigan's *State Flower* has five, pink and white petals with a yellow stamen.

Apple blossoms are classified as **single** (five petals), **semi-double** (six-ten petals), or **double** (more than 10 petals).

In 1897, *Anna Eliza Woodcock* rolled a wheelbarrow full of apple blossoms from her own apple tree two blocks to the Capitol building. She wanted Michigan legislators to choose the fragrant apple blossom to be the official state flower. The legislators agreed with Anna and proudly stated, "Michigan apples have gained a worldwide reputation." They voted to make the apple blossom the State Flower.

More than a century later, Michigan is the second-largest apple producer in the nation.

Connor and Riley visited an apple orchard in Romeo, Michigan to carve the state flower.
They had some apple cider, too.
How far is Romeo from your town?
To find the apple orchard nearest your home, visit
www.michiganapples.com.

Cut an apple in half across the core (with help from an adult) and you'll find a **star shape** inside!

According to **Guinness World Records**™, the largest apple ever plucked from a tree weighed three pounds, two ounces, and was picked in **Caro**, **Michigan**.

Apples are **Michigan's** number one most valuable fruit crop, which has a value of about $150 million annually.

There are over 8 million apple trees in **Michigan**, that cover nearly **42,500 acres** throughout the state.

Apple orchards stretch from the southwest corner of **Michigan** all the way to Traverse City. **Southeast Michigan** is known for apple orchards, too.

More than **20 varieties** of apples grow in **Michigan** orchards. Three longtime favorite varieties are the Red Delicious, Golden Delicious and Gala.

I'm dreaming of **APPLE** - *flavored doggie treats ... YUM!*

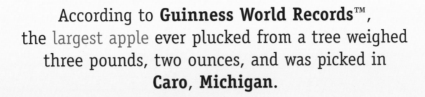

ROBIN - State Bird

After the American Robin was favored in a 1931 Michigan Audubon Society contest to choose a state bird, the Michigan legislature voted to make it official. Legislators called the robin "the best known and best loved of all the birds in the State of Michigan."

Robins are said to be a *sign of spring* and can often be heard singing very early on spring and summer mornings. They can also be found poking around lawns looking for earthworms.

Robins are not really listening for worms when they tilt their head from side to side. Because their eyes are placed so far back on the sides of their heads, they must turn their heads from side to side to look at things.

A SIGN OF SPRING!

Robins are easy to spot! Male robins have slate-gray backs, rusty-red chests and white-speckled throats. Females are gray-brown with pale orange chests.

Both male and female robins feed the young chicks that are born blind and featherless.

Female robins build nests out of mud, grass and twigs. Their nests can be found in trees, shrubs and house gutters.

Female robins lay and incubate **three to five** pale blue eggs that hatch in 12-14 days. The chicks learn to fly and leave the nest after 14-16 days.

Robins return from their winter homes in the southern states and Central American early each spring. In the summertime they can be found in **Michigan** and throughout North American.

Migration Cycle

■ Summer   ■ Year Round   ■ Winter

SPRING

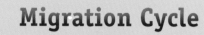

Connor and Riley see lots of robins and other neat birds as they travel around **Michigan**. Connor carved the state bird in his own backyard. Watch for robins and other birds in your neighborhood.

WHITE PINE - State Tree

The *white pine* became the official tree of Michigan in 1955. It was chosen as a symbol of one of Michigan's greatest industries. From 1870 to the early 1900s, Michigan was the number-one lumber producer in the United States.

During this "Green Gold Rush", Michigan lumberjacks cut millions of pine trees worth more than all the gold mined in California. The lumber from these Michigan white pines were used to build growing U.S. cities, towns and railroads.

The white pine, **also known as the** Eastern White Pine, is common throughout Michigan and the northeastern United States. Many people even have white pines growing in their backyards.

The white pine trees found by the first loggers in **Michigan** were hundreds of years old. These trees were tall and straight and most were **80-120 feet tall** with a diameter of **three to four feet.**

"I like the *LOOK* **AND** the *SMELL* of this carving."

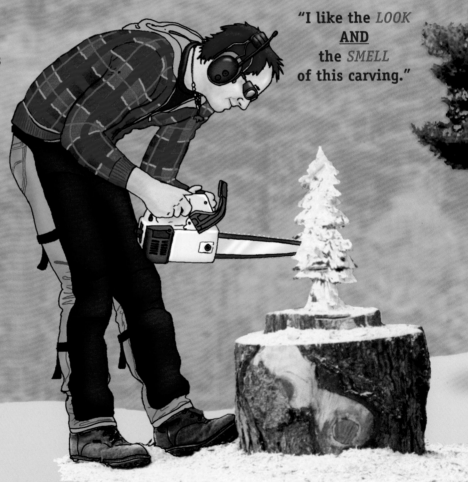

Connor and Riley traveled to **Hartwick Pines State Park** near **Grayling** to see beautiful towering **white pines.** They also saw **Big Wheels** once used by lumberjacks to move heavy logs and visited a lumberjack museum. How far is **Hartwick Pines State Park** from where you live?

Early Native Americans said the white pine *whispered* to them when the wind blew.

1*2*3*4*5!

You can easily spot a white pine tree. It is the only **Michigan evergreen tree** whose needles grow in a bundle, or **cluster of five**. If you have any doubt that the tree you are looking at is a **white pine**, all you have to do is … *count, 1*2*3*4*5!*

The **pine cones** of a white pine tree are long and slender. They are from 3" to 10" long and taper at the end.

Each scale usually bears two winged seeds.

Trees are a renewable resource!

I *really* <u>WOOD</u> like a bone!

BIG WHEELS

Big Wheels were used by loggers to move heavy logs.

BROOK TROUT - State Fish

In 1965, the trout was named as the *state fish*. In 1988, the brook trout was specified by the Michigan legislature as the state fish. The brook trout is native to Michigan and found throughout the state.

Fishing is one of Connor's **favorite outdoor sports. He especially likes fishing for** brook trout, **Michigan's** State Fish.

Connor and Riley **travel to a favorite spot on the** Au Sable River **near** Grayling **to fish and carve the** state fish.

Brook trout **can be found throughout most of the state in many creeks, streams, rivers, lakes and in the Great Lakes.**

FISH PARTS

All fish have several parts in common.

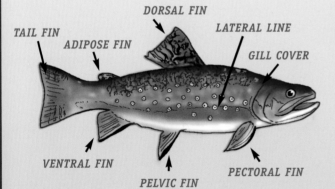

TAIL FIN
ADIPOSE FIN
DORSAL FIN
LATERAL LINE
GILL COVER
VENTRAL FIN
PELVIC FIN
PECTORAL FIN

"My fishing pole is calling my name!"

The* brook trout *is one of* 151 species *of fish found in Michigan.

Connor and Riley **travel** 174 miles **from their home in Oxford, Michigan, to** Grayling **to fish for** brook trout. **How far would you have to travel to fish on Michigan's** Au Sable River?

Fish HATCHERIES ●

Rivers of Michigan

Michigan *fish hatcheries* **hatch up to** 14 species of fish. **Over** 750,000 fish **are planted in the Great Lakes and inland lakes** each year. **Below are the names and locations of the** six **state fish hatcheries.** **See the** *fish eggs symbols* **on the Michigan map at the right.**

1. *Marquette*   2. *Thompson*   3. *Oden*
4. *Platte River*   5. *Harrietta*   6. *Wolf Lake*

HATCHERY

RIVER

FOX   TWO HEARTED
1
2   PIGEON
JORDAN   3   UPPER MANISTEE
BOARDMAN   AU SABLE
BETSIE   4
PERE MARQUETTE   5   RIFLE
PINE
WHITE
ROGUE
FLAT   GRAND RIVER
LOWER KALAMAZOO   6
HURON

Michigan has 36,350 miles of rivers and streams. **Of these, one-third are trout streams. At** 262 miles, **the** Grand River **is the** longest **river in Michigan.**

Connor is no *rookie* at carving a *brookie*!

An average brookie is about seven inches long. A 10-incher would be considered a ...

BIG ONE!

Fly

Anglers use different bait to catch *brook trout* according to water temperature. *Brook trout* usually feed in 55 to 65 degree water. Worms are best in streams and rivers below 50 degrees. Spinning lures also work well up to 60 degrees. For water above 60 degrees, flies are the best choice.

PETOSKEY STONE - STATE STONE

Connor and Riley travel to *Petoskey* on the shores of Lake Michigan to carve the state stone.

In 1965, almost a century after the founding of the city of Petoskey, a bill was signed that made the Petoskey stone Michigan's official State Stone.

Coral
Fossil
Fragment

The Petoskey stone is made up of fossil fragments of corals that existed in Michigan's northern Lower Peninsula about 350 million years ago. Petoskey stones are found in the northern counties of the Lower Peninsula, along the shores of Lake Michigan, Lake Huron and inland lakes. The Petoskey stone is gray with dark spots that show up best when the stone is wet.

Earlier in its life, Hexagonaria, the group of fossil corals that are imprinted on the Petoskey stone, looked like little jellyfish. As they floated around, they would attached themselves to anything hard, mostly to rocks.

I'm a real ROCK HOUND!

*The **Petoskey stone** is a good choice for polishing because it can be polished by hand.*

It's 235 miles from Connor and Riley's home in Oxford to Petoskey. How far do you live from Petoskey?

The possibilities of what can be created with Petoskey stones are limited only by the ... ImAgInAtION!

Petoskeys are primarily calcite. Calcite is soft enough so it can be easily shaped, yet solid enough to take a nice polish. Along the beaches and in most gravels, the stones have already been rounded by glacial and water action making them well suited for *lapidary*.

Most people see their first Petoskey stone in polished form at a gift shop.

Lapidary -
The art of cutting, polishing, or engraving precious stones or gems.

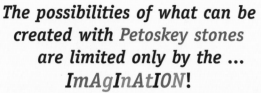

Petoskey, Michigan

"Riley, this Petoskey stone carving is *HOT!*"

onnor uses a torch to add color and depth to the carving of the Petoskey stone.

GREENSTONE - State Gem

Michigan's **State Gem**, **chlorastrolite**, which means **"green star stone"**, was officially adopted in 1972. It is also known by the name greenstone or Isle Royale greenstone.

Most greenstones found today are little green nuggets. When they are polished, you can see the **beautiful** turtleback **pattern**.

Greenstones are very, very old. The stones were created about **one billion years** ago by volcanoes that helped form part of what is now the western Upper Peninsula.

The molten lava solidified, creating rocks full of holes. Later, dissolved minerals passing through the rock caused fine, fibrous crystals to grow at the edge of the holes. They radiated inwards and criss-crossed each other, forming a turtleback pattern.

For many years, greenstones were favorite rocks to be hunted by divers and rock hounds. Now, they are much harder to find. Many rock hounds still scour the **Keweenaw Peninsula's** old copper mines for greenstones and still find small ones.

Greenstones are used in rings and other jewelry. These are becoming more expensive as greenstones become hard and harder to find.

Isle Royale
National Park
Lake Superior

There are only two ways to visit Isle Royale—by boat or by seaplane!

We **MOOSE** be on Isle Royale!

Find Isle Royale on a Michigan map. How long would it take you to get there?

Once upon a time, greenstones the size of golf balls could be found at Isle Royale National Park in Lake Superior. Today, those that can be found are the size of small gravel.

In 1998, after park rangers noticed that Isle Royale's minerals were rapidly disappearing, the park banned the removal of any rocks or minerals from either the island or its waters.

Green Star Stone

"Green is my favorite color!"

Greenstones **range in color from yellowgreen to almost black. They are primarily found in the western Upper Peninsula.**

KALKASKA SAND - STATE SOIL

Kalkaska sand was chosen as **Michigan's** State Soil in 1983. It was the first soil type to be recognized in **Michigan**. Kalkaska sand was first described in 1927 in Kalkaska County, which is the source of its name. It is only found in **Michigan** and covers almost one million acres in 33 of **Michigan's** 83 counties.

The selection process for choosing the **state soil** from more than 400 different soil types began in the 1970s. **Kalkaska sand** was chosen because it is found in both the Upper and Lower Peninsulas and supports the growth of forests, one of **Michigan's** biggest industries. **Kalkaska sand** is also important for growing Christmas trees, potatoes and strawberries.

Why do we have a **state soil**? The **state soil** was chosen to help inform the public about the importance of **Michigan's** soil resources in general. Learning about the **state soil** and **other soils types** found in **Michigan** helps us better understand the **importance of soil** in our daily lives.

Soil is **NOT** an unlimited resource. But with **proper management practices**, soil is a **renewable resource** that can continue to serve the needs of mankind for the future.

Connor and Riley traveled to Kalkaska to learn more about Kalkaska sand. Which direction would you travel to visit Kalkaska?

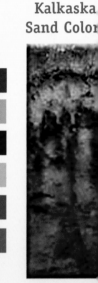

Kalkaska Sand Color

I really *DIG Kalkaska sand!*

"Our State Soil is MUCH MORE than dirt!"

Kalkaska, Michigan

These kids are exploring Kalkaska sand in Kalkaska County. Can you name and locate your county?

Kalkaska sand is **multi-colored**. It is very dark at the surface and gets increasingly lighter as you dig deeper into the ground.

Kalkaska Sand Locations

"Where would we be without soil?"

Most people think soil is dirt. But really, soil includes gravel, sand, silt and clay.

KALKASKA SAND

PAINTED TURTLE - *State Reptile*

The *painted turtle,* **one of** ten **turtle species found in Michigan, was chosen as the** state reptile **in 1995. It was selected to be the** state symbol **after fifth-grade students from** Niles **discovered that Michigan did not have a** state reptile.

Michigan's State Reptile is found throughout the state and North America. This painted turtle lives in wetlands, ponds, lakes, slow-moving rivers and marshes that have soft, muddy bottoms. They usually grow to be six to seven inches long. Scientists are not sure how long painted turtles live, but most probably live for five to ten years. Some painted turtles may live as long as twenty years.

Female painted turtles leave marshes and move into nesting areas to lay eggs from mid-May to early July. They put the eggs in the ground, cover them with dirt using their hind legs and walk away. Eggs incubate throughout the summer and hatch during late August and September. The hatchlings remain in their underground nest for the winter. When the temperature reaches 70 degrees, they leave the nest and head for the nearest body of water.

Actual Size:

hatchling

egg

Connor and Riley visited
Bay City State Recreation Area
to carve this state symbol. Besides painted turtles, they saw many plants, birds and other wildlife. They had a picnic and Connor even went fishing!
(He never leaves home without his fishing pole.)

Find Bay City State Recreation Area on a **Michigan** map. Plan a family outing and spend time outdoors at a state or local park near your home.

Because they are ***cold-blooded,*** *painted turtles* **hibernate**.
During very cold weather, they bury themselves in the mud at the bottom of streams and ponds.

Although it spends most of its time in the water, the painted turtle is a basking turtle. Like the one seen in this picture, the painted turtle can often be found sunbathing on a log or rock on warm sunny days. When it is chilly, painted turtles stay underwater.

This rock was painted to look like a turtle. Find a smooth, round stone and give it a try!

The painted turtle is easily identified by its low, smooth, black or olive *carapace* shell, with red markings along or under the margins.

A **turtle's shell** is important for its survival. Unlike turtles in many cartoons, turtles cannot climb out of their shells.

The *painted turtle* is an *omnivore.*
(It eats both meat and plants.)

Turtles shared the planet with the dinosaurs for millions of years.
The earliest fossil remains of turtles date back 225 million years to the late *Triassic period.*
Today's turtles look very much like their ancient ancestors.

WHITE-TAILED DEER - State

The *white-tailed deer* **was made the state game mammal in 1997 because it is an important Michigan natural and economic resource.**

Though white-tailed deer **are found in every Michigan county,** Connor and Riley **decide to visit a place near Bad Axe in Michigan's "Thumb" to carve this** state symbol.

During hunting season in November, over 800,000 hunters hunt the white-tailed deer in **Michigan**.

It is estimated that more than two million deer roam the state today. They munch on almost everything in their reach including wildflowers, tree seedlings, vegetables and other crops.

Deer have few natural predators and their population has grown larger than the food supply. Many die of starvation. Hunting is important to manage the number of deer and to maintain a healthy deer herd.

Connor and Riley traveled 87 miles from Oxford to Bad Axe to carve this state symbol.

How many miles would you have to travel to get to this place in **Michigan's** "Thumb"?

Game Mammal

A young white-tailed deer is called a **fawn**.

A newborn fawn spends most of the first two weeks of life away from its mother because her scent might attract predators. Mother white-tail stays only long enough to nurse and care for her baby. The fawn's coloring also provides protection from predators by helping it blend in with the surroundings.

A group of fourth graders from Zeeland, Michigan, had the idea to make the **white-tailed deer** the **state game mammal**. Their lobbying efforts made it happen.

Oh, dear! Two million is a lot of DEER!

Kids working together can make things happen!

DWARF LAKE IRIS - State Wildflower

The Dwarf Lake Iris, Michigan's State Wildflower was adopted in 1998. It truly represents the state because it only grows in Michigan. The Dwarf Lake Iris is very rare because it must have just the right combination of light, moisture, soil and temperature to grow and live. It grows in low, wet spots near beaches along the coastlines of northern Lake Michigan and northern and eastern Lake Huron.

Threatened Species

The Dwarf Lake Iris is listed as a *Threatened Species* in **Michigan** and by the Federal Government. This means that it is likely to become *endangered* in the foreseeable future.

The Dwarf Lake Iris is a *Threatened Species* because it is becoming more rare. This is due to the **loss of its habitat**. Off-road vehicles and road and home construction in beach areas are disturbing and taking away the special places where the Dwarf Lake Iris once grew.

Pretty to look at but
DO NOT touch or pick!

Usually, the Dwarf Lake Iris does not bloom before Memorial Day. It is most often found growing in thick patches beneath cedar trees near shoreline backdunes.

To carve the Dwarf Lake Iris, Connor and Riley travel across the *Mackinac Bridge*. They head for Cedarville in the Le Cheneaux Islands of the eastern Upper Peninsula. In addition to the state wildflower, they see beautiful scenery, wildlife and lots of wooden boats and boathouses.

Northern Michigan Shorelines

The state wildflower only grows on the northern shoreline of Lake Michigan and the northern and eastern shoreline of Lake Huron.

The Dwarf Lake Iris is purple and a lot smaller than other irises. It is only six to eight inches tall, with a flower that is 1.5 to two inches in diameter.

Picking the Dwarf Lake Iris or any state wildflower is against the law.

MASTODON - State Fossil

The *Mastodon*, a long-extinct mammal, was named the state fossil by the Michigan legislature in 2002. This happened because students at Slauson Middle School in Ann Arbor conducted a state fossil campaign. When the students reached their goal, they declared, *"The mighty Mastodon, hairy and colossal, has become our state fossil.*

University of Michigan Museum of Natural History (Mastodon exhibit)

This magnificent creature once lived throughout Michigan and North America.

The mastodon disappeared about 10,000 years ago, but its bones are still being studied by paleontologis (pay-lee-on-TAHL-uhjists), or fossil scientists. **Mastodon** fossils have been found throughout the Great Lak **Region** with over 250 discoveries in **Michigan**. Mastodons were large members of the elephant family. They stood as much as 10 feet high at the shoulder. **Mastodon fossils** are most often found in regions that were forested during the Late Pliocene and Pleistocene epochs (4 million - 10,000 years ago). The only known **mastodon trackway** was uncovered near Saline, Michigan. A cast of this trackway is on display at *The University of Michigan Exhibit Museum of Natural History* in Ann Arbor.

Connor (Riley couldn't come along on this trip.) visited *The University of Michigan Exhibit Museum of Natural History* in *Ann Arbor* to get ideas for carving this **state symbol**. At the museum, he was able to see one of the most complete **mastodon** skeletons ever found. It was discovered in 1944 near *Owoss*

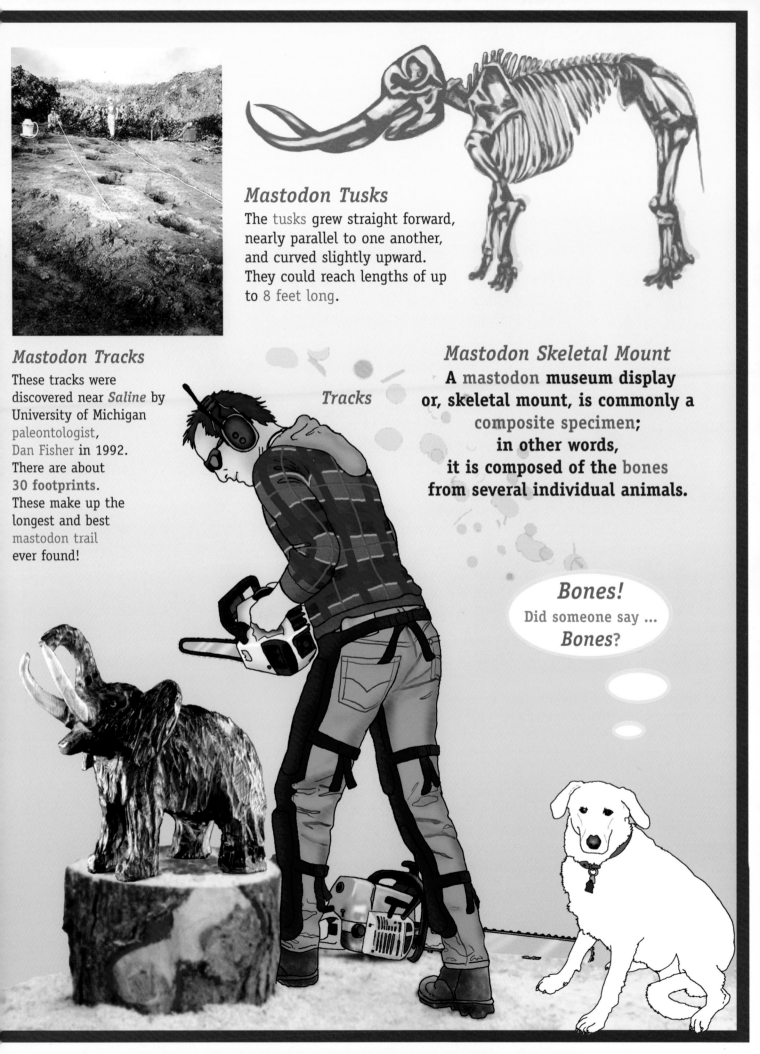

Mastodon Tusks

The tusks grew straight forward, nearly parallel to one another, and curved slightly upward. They could reach lengths of up to 8 feet long.

Mastodon Tracks

These tracks were discovered near *Saline* by University of Michigan paleontologist, Dan Fisher in 1992. There are about 30 footprints. These make up the longest and best mastodon trail ever found!

Tracks

Mastodon Skeletal Mount

A mastodon museum display or, skeletal mount, is commonly a composite specimen; in other words, it is composed of the bones from several individual animals.

Bones!
Did someone say ...
Bones?

MICHIGAN LIGHTHOUSES

Fort Gratiot - First Michigan Lighthouse

Lighthouses **are not official** state symbols, **but Michigan is known for its** lighthouses **and has more than any other state. Michigan touches four of the five** Great Lakes, **so** lighthouses **have been important in the history and shipping industry of the state.**

Lighthouses are navigational aids. They help ships find their way in storms, at night and in fog. They also mark nearly every port as well as dangerous reefs and shoals. In the past, the United States Coast Guard managed lighthouses. With new, modern technology, many lighthouses have been eliminated or sold to individuals or groups.

Connor and Riley **enjoy visiting Michigan** lighthouses. **They traveled to** *Port Huron* **to see the** Fort Gratiot Light, **Michigan's oldest** lighthouse.

A Fresnel lens used in lighthouses magnified the light using a series of glass prisms!

Many lighthouses **have been sold to individuals. Big Bay Point Light on Lake Superior in the Upper Peninsula is now a bed and breakfast.**

Over 300 lighthouses are located along the five Great Lakes.

Tri-Centennial State Park and Harbor

After visiting the oldest lighthouse, Connor and Riley traveled to Tri-Centennial State Park in Detroit to see the newest lighthouse. Michigan's newest lighthouse is located in the first urban state park in Michigan. The 31 acres along the banks of the Detroit River are a green oasis in the midst of Michigan's largest city.

Due to modern technology there are only a few lighthouse keepers left in the United States.

Built in 2004, the 63-foot Harbor Safety Lighthouse marks the harbor entrance of *Tri-Centennial State Park* in Detroit. It is a scaled-down replica of the Tawas Point Lighthouse in Tawas, Michigan.

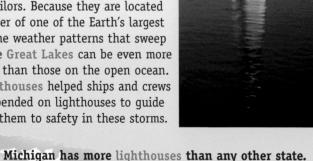

Michigan Lighthouses

The Great Lakes have always presented a special challenge for sailors. Because they are located near the center of one of the Earth's largest landmasses, the weather patterns that sweep across the Great Lakes can be even more violent than those on the open ocean. Lighthouses helped ships and crews depended on lighthouses to guide them to safety in these storms.

Michigan has more lighthouses **than any other state.**

"I see the light!"

For over a hundred years, *Michigan* and Great Lakes sailors depended on *lighthouses*.

Livingstone Memorial Lighthouse **built in 1929.**

After visiting the *Tri-Centennial Harbor Light*, Connor and Riley drove across the Belle Isle Bridge to see the *Livingstone Memorial Lighthouse*. Located on the north end of Belle Isle in the Detroit River, it is the only light in the nation constructed from marble.

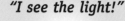
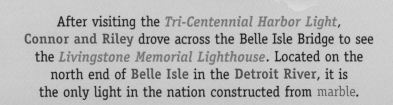

CONNOR'S GALLERY (

APPLE BLOSSOM
STATE FLOWER

WHITE-TAILED DEER
STATE GAME MAMMAL

PETOSKEY STONE
STATE STONE

Welcome to Connor's Gallery of Michigan Symbols!

ROBIN
STATE BIRD

WHITE PINE
STATE TREE

MICHIGAN SYMBOLS

PAINTED TURTLE
STATE REPTILE

GREENSTONE
STATE GEM

BROOK TROUT
STATE FISH

MASTODON
STATE FOSSIL

KALKASKA SAND
STATE SOIL

Connor is an AMAZING Wood Carver!

DWARF LAKE IRIS
STATE WILDFLOWER
(Threatened Species)

RILEY
K9!

About the Author and Illustrator

I'm Riley, Connor's best friend.

Gary Elzerman - As a young boy, Gary was dyslexic. Learning was neither easy nor much fun, but with determination and persistence he made it through school. Years later, Gary wanted his son to have a more positive school experience and understand that learning can be fun. When his son had to learn about Michigan's state symbols, Gary got the idea for this book. He wanted to show his children and others that with effort, determination and a positive attitude even the things that are the hardest for us can be accomplished.

When he sets out to do something -- look out! Gary has set goals and re-invented himself several times. He has been a successful carpenter, executive chef, ice carver, store owner and most recently an award winning chainsaw artist. With only word-of-mouth advertising, over 6,000 Michiganders now own a piece of Gary's custom chainsaw art! There are about 28 chain-saw artists in Michigan and only about 250 in the USA. Gary's art is in such demand that he usually has a list of more than 30 requests for commissioned pieces. Gary lives in Oxford, Michigan with his wife, son, daughter and loyal canine friend.

Mark Herrick is the illustrator of the award-winning Michigan L.A.P.'s™ Program, Michigan Outdoor Explorers Club newsletter, *ROCK U.S.A.* ™ *and the American Way, Buck Wilder's Small Twig Hiking and Camping Guide* and *Buck Wilder's Small Fry Fishing Guide*. A piece of his artwork traveled to the Space Station Mir with Astronaut Jerry Linenger. In 2000, Mark was chosen to create the White House Easter Egg for Michigan. Mark lives in Holly, Michigan.

COMCAST FOUNDATION AND LITERACY PARTNERSHIP OF SOUTHEAST MICHIGAN

CERTIFICATE OF APPRECIATION

GLORIA BODDY

IN RECOGNITION OF YOUR COMMITMENT TO LITERACY

Cathryn Weiss

CATHRYN WEISS

JUNE 6, 2006

Comcast
FOUNDATION

LITERACY PARTNERSHIP of Southeast Michigan

Macomb Literacy Partners
Oakland Literacy Council
ProLiteracy Detroit